STEM Junior
ENGINEERING

KINGFISHER
LONDON & NEW YORK

KINGFISHER
LONDON & NEW YORK

Text and design copyright © Toucan Books Ltd. 2020
Illustrations copyright © Simon Basher 2020
www.basherscience.com

First published 2020 in the United States by Kingfisher
120 Broadway, New York, NY 10271
Kingfisher is an imprint of Macmillan Children's Books, London

Author: Jonathan O'Callaghan
Consultant: Christine Cunningham
Editor: Anna Southgate
Designer: Leah Germann
Proofreader: Richard Beatty
Indexer: Marie Lorimer

Dedicated to Noel, Natalia, Agi, and Art

Distributed in the U.S. and Canada by Macmillan,
120 Broadway, New York, NY 10271

Library of Congress Cataloging-in-Publication Data has been applied for.

ISBN: 978-0-7534-7560-7 (Hardcover)
ISBN: 978-0-7534-7556-0 (Paperback)

Kingfisher books are available for special promotions and premiums.
For details contact: Special Markets Department, Macmillan, 120 Broadway,
New York, NY 10271

For more information, please visit www.kingfisherbooks.com

Printed in China
9 8 7 6 5 4 3 2 1
1TR/0420/WKT/UG/128MA

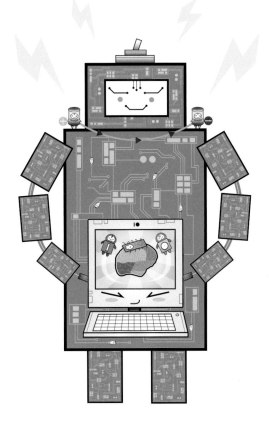

Contents

Ingenious Engineering

Wow! That's a mouthful, but it has to be said. Ingenious basically means "super smart, inventive, imaginative, and creative" — all the things the colorful characters in this book have in common. So what is engineering? Well, it's a world in which people use scientific know-how to design and create great stuff.

Almost everything people make has been engineered. That includes roads, bridges, and skyscrapers, but also the protective Band-Aid you stick over a scrape on your knee and the stretchy socks you're wearing! But this is just scratching the surface. The world of engineering is HUGE, full of characters working hard to find ways to make things stronger or stretchier, waterproof or super lightweight, and more. Come on, let's find out what they have to say.

Research

Brainstorm

Design

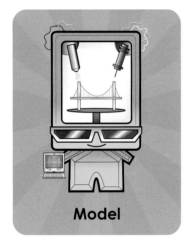

Model

Test

Improve

Lab Rats

Come and meet the Lab Rats. These characters will tell
you all you need to know about the engineering design
cycle. This is a series of steps that every engineer needs to
follow as part of building something. It all kicks off with
Research and Brainstorm. Creative Design and Model
develop things further, and Test and Improve
wrap things up. Step into the laboratory and let
your engineering journey begin.

Research

★ Fact Finder

THE BIG IDEA

Careful and detailed investigation into a subject. Engineers use research to learn about the **criteria** and **constraints** of a project.

Every engineering job starts with me — Research. I can be hard work, but you won't get far without me. Say you want to build a bridge. What different styles of bridges are there? What purposes do they serve? What materials are they made of? Um . . . how do you even build a bridge?

So many questions! My job is to ask these kinds of questions and many more. Above all, I need to know two things: What does a design need to do? And what could get in the way of making that happen? I dig around and, little by little, I gather a huge amount of information to complete this first step of the engineering cycle.

- ⦿ Researchers need to consider "ergonomics" — how the design of something best suits human users

- ⦿ Building projects use surveys to measure the shape of a plot of land

⚡ SAY WHAT? ⚡

Criteria: In research, what a design needs to do or achieve.

Constraint: Anything that limits what can be done or achieved when designing something.

✳ REAL WORLD VIEW ✳

Engineers use many types of research. These include looking things up on the Internet, talking to experts, and testing things in the laboratory. A laboratory (or lab) is a room full of equipment for doing experiments.

Brainstorm

★ Group Thinker

THE BIG IDEA

To come up with many different ideas, usually in order to find a **solution** to a particular problem.

So my pal Research has all the information, but what now? Well, you need me, Brainstorm. I'm the smart-thinking stage of the cycle. I use what Research has learned in order to do some creative, out-of-the-box thinking.

I give shape to an idea, suggesting many different ways something can be done. Take all that information Research has. How high should your bridge be? How long? Will it be raised on columns, or can it hang from up high? What's best to build with: Wood or Concrete or Steel? Ask me! My crazy ideas get the juices flowing and might just lead to something really unique.

- Brainstorming is normally done in groups of up to 10 people

- The average person has 70,000 thoughts per day!

⚡ SAY WHAT? ⚡

Solution: One possible answer to a given question or problem.

✳ APPLYING SCIENCE ✳

Brainstorming relies on a group of people sharing their ideas. Anything goes! It helps to write the ideas on a board so everyone can talk about them a little more. That way, the group figures out which ideas are the best.

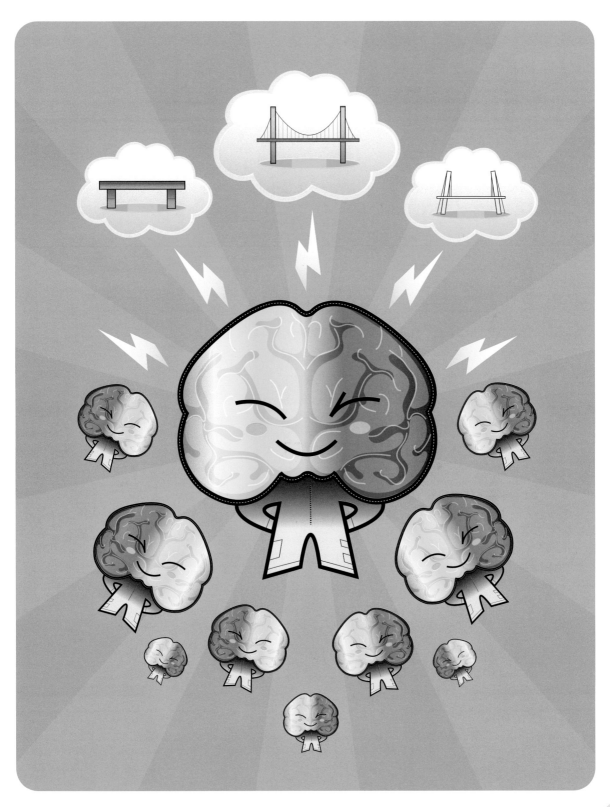

Design
★ Sketch Maker

THE BIG IDEA

The stage in the engineering cycle when all the details are worked out in a drawing or **sketch**.

Hey! I'm Design, the part of the cycle that puts Brainstorm's bright ideas into action. I'm a creative type, but I have a practical side, too. I figure out how an engineering project is actually going to work.

I like to sketch things out to see all the details coming together. Looking at your bridge, I'd work on paper or a computer to show different angles — a side view, a view from above, even a slice straight through the middle. I'd figure out how strong it needs to be (to carry trains, cars, or people) and how it's going to stay up. Of course, I'd make sure it looked mega-fantastic, too.

- ◉ When designers produce a diagram with lots of details about a project, it's called a blueprint

- ◉ A "sectional drawing" shows a structure sliced in half, so you can see inside it

⚡ SAY WHAT? ⚡

Sketch: In engineering, to make a diagram or drawing that shows the various parts of a project that you're hoping to build.

✳ APPLYING SCIENCE ✳

Many designers use computers to help them do their work. We call this computer-aided design, or CAD. A computer can help a designer produce more accurate drawings.

Model
★ Miniature Marvel

THE BIG IDEA

A small, three-dimensional (3-D) version of something. Its three dimensions are length (or width), height, and depth.

My pal Design does great work sketching out the details of an engineering project, but how can you find out if those plans are going to work once the thing is built? Well, you make me, Model, a **scaled-down** version of the finished thing.

Engineers build me using basic materials or a 3-D printer. I can show them how their design will work and what it can do. Depending on the type of project, engineers might even build a prototype from Design's drawings. This is a **full-scale model** that actually functions, so that engineers can test all aspects of the design.

- Architects make detailed scaled-down models of their designs

- Product designers often make a prototype — say for a smartphone or even a hairbrush

SAY WHAT?

Scaled-down: A version of something that is identical in every way but several sizes smaller.

Full-scale model: A model that is exactly the same size as the real thing.

SCIENCE NOW

Engineers don't always build a physical model. Sometimes they create one on a computer, using virtual graphics. It serves the same purpose: to test whether or not a design works. It saves time and can be changed easily!

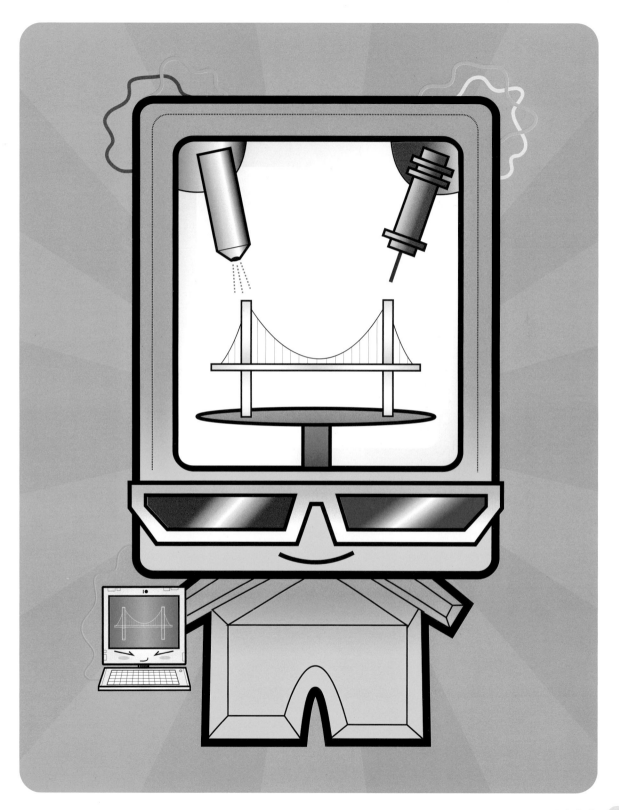

Test

★ Careful Checker

THE BIG IDEA

To carry out a series of actions or experiments to see how well something works.

So Design draws sketches and Model gives them the 3-D treatment, but does it all actually work? Use me, Test, and you're sure to find out.

I work closely with Model to see how something will function. With your bridge, my job is to make it as safe as possible for things to go across it and under it. I might check how much weight it can handle, for example, or what happens to it when there's a storm. I'm here to spot ways in which the bridge might fail to do its job. Now, where's that wind machine?

⊙ Fabrics for raincoats are tested to see how waterproof they are

⊙ Zippers on clothing are tested over and over again for their **durability**

⊙ Engineers use heavy weights to find the "breaking point" of something

✳ **APPLYING SCIENCE** ✳

Car engineers use "crash test dummies." These clever devices look and behave like the human body. Engineers crash prototype cars into obstacles with the dummies inside them. It means they can test the safety of a car without anyone getting hurt.

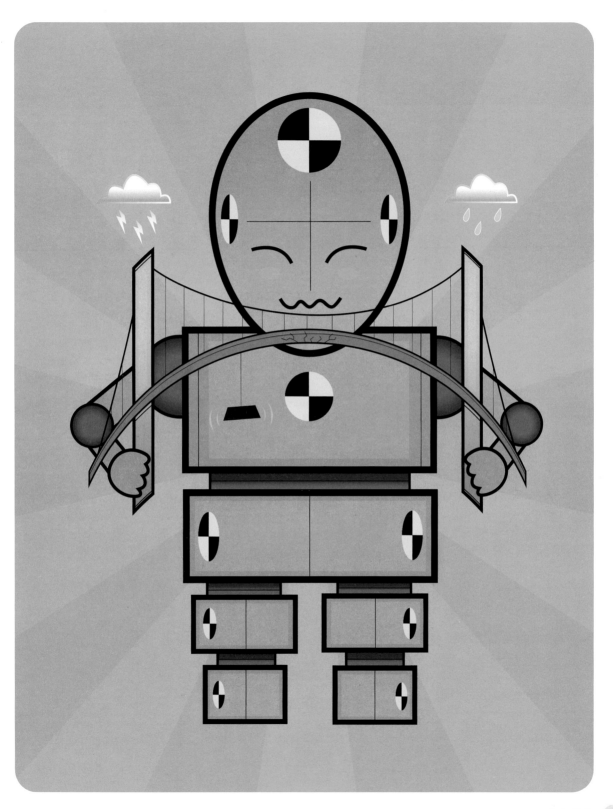

Improve
★ Ultimate Upgrader

THE BIG IDEA
Making **adjustments** to the design of something so that it runs more smoothly.

So Test has been hard at work, setting Model all kinds of challenges. Now what? Well, not all designs are perfect the first time around, and that's where I come in — Improve.

I'm an important piece of the puzzle in any engineering project. I take a look at Test's results and see if I can do anything to make Design and Model work better. I'm a hard taskmaster and could go a few rounds with Model before I'm satisfied. I might even make Design refine a sketch here and there. With my stage of the process, the engineering design cycle is complete. Well, what are you waiting for? Build that bridge of yours!

- One of the world's tallest buildings, the Burj Khalifa, in Dubai, is earthquake proof

- Sports clothing often has features that improve performance, such as holes to let air flow in and keep you cool

SAY WHAT?

Adjustment: A small change that is made to something such as a machine or a process.

✳ APPLYING SCIENCE ✳

Some buildings need to be able to withstand earthquakes. To do this, they are often designed to rock from side to side. This means that if the ground starts to shake, the building can ride out a small-to-medium-size earthquake and still manage to stay upright.

**Mechanical
Engineering**

**Chemical
Engineering**

**Civil
Engineering**

**Industrial
Engineering**

**Electrical
Engineering**

**Agricultural
Engineering**

**Transportation
Engineering**

**Environmental
Engineering**

**Biomedical
Engineering**

**Materials
Engineering**

The Specialists

The world of engineering is so VARIED that it's organized into different types, or "fields," each with its own Specialist in this chapter. For example, Mechanical Engineering focuses on machines and things with moving parts, while bridges and skyscrapers belong to Civil Engineering. Environmental Engineering develops solutions to pollution, and Biomedical Engineering wants to improve your health. You won't believe how smart these characters are, and they can't wait to tell you more.

Mechanical Engineering
Machine Maker

THE BIG IDEA

This field of engineering deals with every type of tool, engine, and machine — big and small.

I'm Mechanical Engineering. The oldest type of engineering, I specialize in machines. I just love to play with gizmos and systems that have moving parts.

I'm talking physics here! That's the science that studies how things move. I'm fascinated with the way machines operate and the **forces** that drive them. I need to know about the materials that things are made of. I need to know how to assemble a machine to make it operate with the greatest **efficiency**. And I need to know about everything from from robots to radiators and engines to elevators.

- The ancient Greek inventor Archimedes devised a pump for drawing water — a design that's still in use today

- Mechanical engineers use plenty of clever devices, including levers, gears, screws, pumps, and engines

SAY WHAT?

Force: An amount of energy that causes an object to move in a certain direction when the force is applied.

Efficiency: The good use of time and energy while performing a task.

TOP ENGINEER

Famous mechanical engineers include Serbian-American inventor Nikola Tesla. He pioneered our use of radio and electricity in the late 19th and early 20th centuries, and even came up with the idea of a smartphone in 1901.

Chemical Engineering
⭐ Matter Fan

THE BIG IDEA

A field of engineering that transforms raw materials into things that we use every day, such as bottles and clothes.

My name is Chemical Engineering, and I specialize in "matter" — the stuff everything in the universe is made of! You know Earth is bursting with all sorts of raw materials — metals, rocks, soils? Well, I like to know what **chemicals** these things are made of. Then I can figure out how to use them to make useful things that you can use every day!

You'll often find me in a laboratory testing out this and that. For example, I might be developing a new type of plastic for your school lunchbox. Or I could be investigating materials for making longer-lasting shoes for running!

- Chemical engineers develop textiles, ceramics, and plastics

- More than 80,000 chemicals are used around the world

SAY WHAT?

Chemical: Any substance found in the world that is made up of matter. It can be a solid, liquid, or gas.

✳ GREAT INVENTION ✳

Perhaps one of the most amazing inventions to come from chemical engineering is safe drinking water. Find out more on page 68.

Civil Engineering
Cool Constructor

THE BIG IDEA

Engineering that helps large structures and buildings, such as bridges, houses, and sewers, stand the test of time.

Allow me to introduce myself. A master builder extraordinaire, I'm Civil Engineering, and I'm very pleased to meet you. Hello!

"Infrastructure" is the name of my game. It means I specialize in all the facilities that help make modern living run smoothly. I build roads and railroads, bridges, tunnels, and dams, and houses and skyscrapers. My secret lies in setting a firm **foundation**, and then away I go. And I don't just do the stuff you can see, but the stuff you can't see, too. This includes the pipes that bring clean water to your faucets. (And the pipes that carry your toilet waste away. Yuck!)

- The longest and deepest rail tunnel is the 35-mile (57-km) Gotthard high-speed rail link under the Alps in Switzerland

- Human-made Palm Jumeirah island in Dubai is built entirely from sand and rocks (and no concrete or steel)

SAY WHAT?

Foundation: The part of a building that goes into the ground and that supports the entire weight of the building above it.

TOP ENGINEER

Isambard Kingdom Brunel is a famous British civil engineer who lived in the 1800s. He built the world's first iron ship to cross the Atlantic, the SS *Great Britain*, and revolutionized how we build railroads, bridges, tunnels, and more.

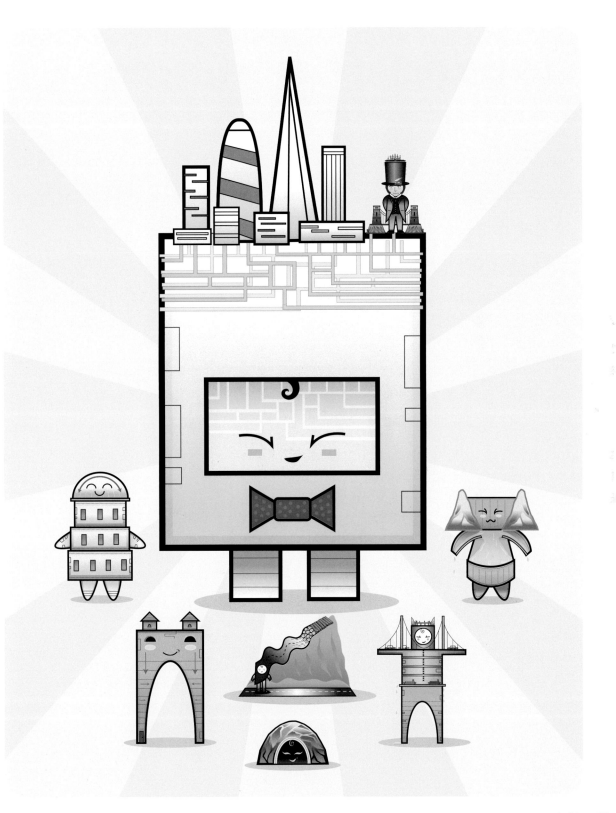

Industrial Engineering
Inspector Improver

THE BIG IDEA

This field of engineering is concerned with large-scale production and manufacturing **processes**.

Right at home inside a manufacturing plant, I'm Industrial Engineering. I'm a no-nonsense, hard-working type of engineering with a passion for improving machines and their production processes.

Take a car plant. Sure, I'll look for ways to make that car more cheaply and in less time. But I'll also work on making the plant machinery and processes more efficient. Mine is a dangerous world, and I take measures to keep my human workers as safe as possible. I also work with Environmental Engineering to keep the manufacturing process nice and **green**.

- In 1913, American carmaker Henry Ford invented the factory assembly line

- Today's robotic machines can work longer than humans because they never get tired

SAY WHAT?

Process: A series of actions or steps taken in order to reach a particular result.

Green: Kind to the environment.

TOP ENGINEER

Canadian inventor Elijah McCoy was the brains behind something that makes all our machinery work — lubrication! In in the late 1800s, he came up with ways to make sure machinery kept running and didn't stick. Our machinery has been running smoothly ever since.

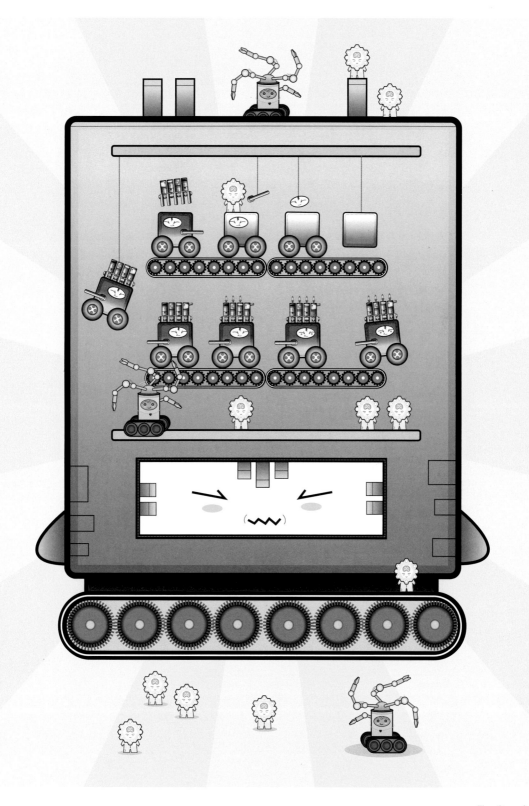

Electrical Engineering

★ Power Pal

THE BIG IDEA

This kind of engineering focuses on using electricity to make things work. It includes anything that uses a circuit or wires.

No crossed wires here! My name is Electrical Engineering. I work with electricity to make gadgets and gizmos work. It's as simple as that. Look around your house and you'll see my work in everything from the TV to the bathroom light.

I often use a web of wires (called a circuit) to channel a **current** around an electrical device — say a computer or a smartphone. If wired correctly, all the different parts of the device work properly when you switch it on. Batteries make some of your toys work. I store energy in these clever things so that Mechanical Engineering can use them to get those machines running.

◉ The ancient Greeks discovered a type of electricity in 600 BC by rubbing fur on amber (fossilized tree resin)

◉ The whole world uses twice as much electricity now as it did in 1990

SAY WHAT?

Current: A flow of electricity through a wire or circuit. It transfers energy from one area of a device or system to another.

GREAT INVENTION

In 1799, Italian inventor Alessandro Volta made the world's first battery from the metals copper and zinc. Others had used frogs' legs to produce "animal electricity," but Volta proved that the source of electricity was the metals, not the animal.

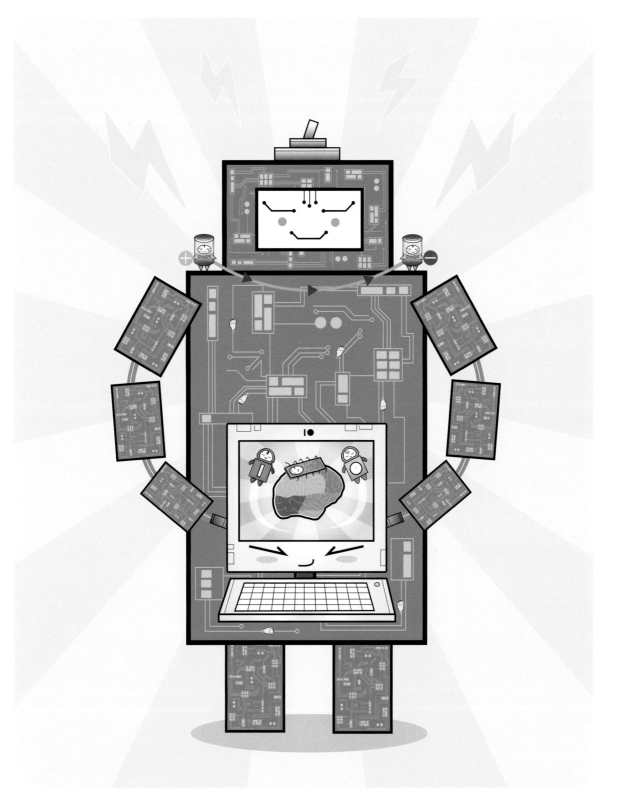

Agricultural Engineering
Great Grower

THE BIG IDEA

Engineering that focuses on growing things. This includes food, as well as plant materials for making things.

Hi, I'm Agricultural Engineering, and I specialize in growing things. Just think about all the food you eat. I'll have played a role in putting it on your plate. I also help grow plants that are useful for making things — cotton for clothes, say.

My job is more complicated than sowing seeds and feeding cows! I have to think about all the processes involved. With food **crops**, I might figure out the best conditions for growing or help keep plants pest-free. One day I'll be testing soil samples in the lab, the next I could be designing a new machine for plowing fields. It's all food for thought . . .

- Agricultural engineering wasn't taught until 1903, but farming began as long as 12,000 years ago

- Desert locusts swarm in their millions and can eat their way through entire crops in a matter of minutes

SAY WHAT?

Crop: A plant that's grown in large quantities, usually for food. Fruits, vegetables, and cereals such as wheat are all types of crops.

TOP ENGINEER

In 1910, the German agricultural engineer Fritz Haber found a way to take nitrogen from Earth's atmosphere and turn it into food for plants. We call it fertilizer. Without it we wouldn't be able to grow everything we need.

Transportation Engineering
Go-Getter

THE BIG IDEA

Engineering that develops vehicles and routes that can transport people and cargo from one place to another.

If getting from A to B is your thing, then come with me, Transportation Engineering! I'm the engineer that comes up with all the cool ways to travel around the world, whether on a bike, in a car, or by plane.

I don't just design **vehicles**. Oh no, I also make all kinds of calculations to find the best ways of getting vehicles from one place to the next. I might devise a road or rail network, for example, seeing whether it's quicker to go through a city or around it. I've already conquered land, sea, and air. What's next? Oh yeah, space!

- The world's first airplane took flight in 1903, in North Carolina

- The world's longest railroad stretches 5,800 miles (9,300 km); called the Trans-Siberian Railway, it runs through Russia from Moscow to Vladivostok

SAY WHAT?

Vehicle: A mode of transportation that carries people or cargo from one place to another, often using engines and wheels or another form of movement.

FAST-FORWARD

Engineers have developed a type of train that doesn't run on tracks! It's called a maglev train, and it uses powerful magnets to hover above a track. The train can reach mega-high speeds and doesn't cause any pollution.

Environmental Engineering

Green Champion

THE BIG IDEA

A field of engineering that looks at ways to make the world a less polluted place.

If you want to make the world around you (a.k.a. the environment) a better place, join me. I'm Environmental Engineering, and I'm on a mission to keep our planet fresh and clean.

Take water. I'm always looking for ways to make that vital liquid safer to drink. What about air? Humans rely on **fossil fuels**, but they produce pollution — you know, substances that cause harm to the environment. I want to see people taking measures to improve the quality of the air your breathe. This sees me looking for greener ways to power the planet (see Renewable Energy on page 92).

- Earth is getting hotter every year. If we do nothing about it, our planet could be 7°F (4°C) hotter by 2100

- Plastic bottles can be recycled to make new things, such as fabric for T-shirts

SAY WHAT?

Fossil fuel: A type of fuel that formed thousands or millions of years ago and is found in the ground. Oil and gas are fossil fuels.

SCIENCE NOW

Engineers in many countries around the world are trying to use less oil, and drivers are switching to electric cars. The world also recycles more year after year. But there's still much more to do!

Biomedical Engineering
Amazing Enhancer

THE BIG IDEA

Engineering that looks at ways to improve the health of patients, often with the help of robots and machines.

Most of my Specialist pals deal with lifeless objects. Not me! I'm Biomedical Engineering, and I investigate ways to keep both humans and animals healthy.

A good deal of my work is machine based. I design robots that can perform surgery, and I devise ways of peering inside the body to see what's going on (think X-ray and **MRI**). I also help design **prosthetic** and robotic limbs. Oh, and have you seen my cool wrist-worn fitness tracker? It shows me how many steps I take in a day and the number of calories I burn as I do so! Hey, come jog with me!

- A 3,000-year-old prosthetic toe was found on an Egyptian mummy

- Robotic arms were first used in surgery in 1985

SAY WHAT?

MRI: Magnetic resonance imaging, a technique for forming pictures of the inside of the body.

Prosthetic: An artificial body part such as an arm, a leg, or even a heart.

APPLYING SCIENCE

Age-old biomedical inventions include thermometers, which measure your body temperature, and stethoscopes, which can hear your heart beating. Using the very latest technology, cochlear implants help deaf people hear sound.

Materials Engineering

⭐ Mega Maker

THE BIG IDEA

A field of engineering that looks at creating and using different **materials**.

Everything is made of something, and that's what I'm all about. I'm Materials Engineering. I find new and interesting ways to use the different substances engineers have at their fingertips, such as glass, metal, and plastic. I'm also pretty skilled at creating new materials, such as Teflon (a coating that makes cooking pans "nonstick").

With an eye on the future, I've also started to delve into really young branches of science. For example, I'm interested in providing materials for mega clever, ultra-speedy supercomputers. And I love the nano world, where things are so small you can't see them with the naked eye.

- ◉ Materials engineering is very new; it began in the 1940s

- ◉ Iron and silicon are two of the most commonly used materials on Earth

SAY WHAT?

Material: A chemical, or mix of chemicals, in the form of a solid object. Some materials are natural, but others can only be made by human beings.

APPLYING SCIENCE

A really exciting new material is graphene. It is the thinnest material known to humans, but it's super strong and even conducts electricity! Find out more on page 64.

Wood

Paper

Glass

Concrete

Steel

Aluminum

Plastic

Ceramic

Textile

Adhesive

Graphene

Cool Stuff

These Cool Stuff characters get everywhere —
you use most of them every single day of your life.
From ancient heroes Wood, Paper, and Glass to
modern-day marvels such as Graphene, each one
of these clever materials shines in its own special way.
Where would you be without Textile, Concrete, and
Steel? Naked and without a school to go to for
starters! Come and meet the team and find
out why the stuff that surrounds you is
so unbelievably cool.

Wood

★ Lumber Chum

THE BIG IDEA

The tough stuff that trees make as they grow. Wood is used for constructing buildings and making furniture.

One of the first materials ever used for building things, I have an ancient history. I'm Wood, the stuff trees are made of. Yes, I am old, but I'm still in demand today. I come as many different types, from hard oak to soft pine. And I'm useful because I'm really tough.

Chop me up to use as **timber** for building houses or for making smaller things such as tables and chairs. I last a long time, sometimes hundreds of years, and I'm cheap to use, too. Just be sure to replace me when you chop me down. That way there will be trees on the planet forever.

- ◉ Wood was used to build houses around 10,000 years ago

- ◉ There are at least three trillion trees on planet Earth; that's more than 400 trees per person

SAY WHAT?

Timber: Wood that has been chopped down and prepared for use in construction. Also known as lumber.

FAST-FORWARD

When humans first started using wood, they chopped down large numbers of trees. Trees help the environment, so nowadays when humans chop trees down, they plant new ones to replace them. This helps Earth keep its precious forests.

Paper
⭐ Fiber Provider

THE BIG IDEA

A material made by pressing **plant fiber** into thin sheets and drying them. Its uses include writing, printing, and packaging.

Ha! I bet you use me all the time, but have no idea where I come from? Well, just like my friend Wood, I come from trees! I'm Paper — you use me to write and draw on.

I'm made of plant fiber. Plants get crushed up and mixed with water to make a soft, wet mush called pulp. Spread the pulp out really thin, leave it to dry, and — bingo — you've got paper! Just like Wood, I have ancient roots, and I was originally made by hand. Now that I have so many uses, I'm made by machine. Just look around and you'll see me everywhere — as books, candy wrappers, money, toilet paper . . . and more.

- ◉ The ancient Egyptians used an early form of paper called papyrus

- ◉ Paper can be recycled; an old newspaper could be made into paper party cups and straws

SAY WHAT?

Plant fiber: Part of a plant made of cells, usually in the form of a thin thread. Lots of fiber joined together can be pressed to make paper.

GREAT INVENTION

In 1493, German blacksmith Johannes Gutenberg invented the printing press. It featured metal letters arranged in a frame. The letters were covered in ink and pressed against paper to make a page of a book. The process could be repeated over and over.

Glass

★ Amazing Glazing

THE BIG IDEA

A rigid, solid material made from sand. It's used for making windows (glazing) and other things you can see through.

Here's something amazing. Ready for it? I'm Glass and I. Am. Made. Of. SAND! Can you believe that?

Glassmakers heat up sand to really high temperatures. As the sand cools down, it becomes a sort of stiff liquid — that's me. Usually see-through, I am pretty easy and cheap to make in large amounts. Sand is melted inside a big cauldron, called a **furnace**. In my liquid form, I am poured into molds to make different shapes — think drinking glasses, vases for flowers, and light bulbs. You'll also see me around the place as windows, TV screens, and so much more.

- ◉ Glass was first made in 3500 BC in Egypt; they used it to make colorful beads

- ◉ When lightning hits sand it can turn it into glass

SAY WHAT?

Furnace: A structure used for heating materials such as sand or iron (see page 52) to extremely high temperatures. A furnace is normally gas-powered.

SCIENCE NOW

There's a type of glass that's so strong it can stop bullets! It is made by combining layers of glass and plastic. The plastic in bulletproof glass absorbs the energy of a fired bullet so that the glass doesn't break.

Concrete

⭐ Mega Builder

THE BIG IDEA

A strong building material, concrete is made from rock, sand, and gravel mixed with **cement** and water.

I'm everywhere, but what do you know about me? Well, I'm Concrete, a mixture of water, sand, gravel, and a type of glue called cement. The water mixes me up, and the cement holds me together. I'm a sloppy mess when wet, but I can be molded into almost any shape, and I'm mega hard once I dry out.

I've been around for centuries, and builders love to use me for all kinds of construction work, including houses, bridges, dams, and skyscrapers. And, you know, I heard a rumor that I might just be one of the most important inventions EVER. I'm not going to argue with that!

- ◉ The ancient Romans made a type of concrete using volcanic ash

- ◉ Concrete is the second-most-used material on Earth after water

- ◉ The Three Gorges Dam in China is the world's biggest concrete structure

SAY WHAT?

Cement: A mixture of limestone and clay. It creates a sticky glue-like paste when water is added to it.

TOP ENGINEER

Modern concrete was invented by British engineer John Smeaton in 1756. He used pebbles, powdered brick, and cement to create a basic mixture.

Steel
⭐ Super Supporter

THE BIG IDEA

A tough metal that's widely used in the construction of buildings, as well as smaller items.

I'm Steel. An **alloy** of iron and carbon, I have awesome strength. I'm made by heating iron to very high temperatures in a furnace and adding carbon, usually in the form of a rock called **coke**. The mega-hot gloop (molten steel) is cooled and turned into useful sheets of me!

I get around! I pair up with Concrete to build skyscrapers and bridges, but you'll also find me in ships, railroad tracks, and cars. I even make really small things such as pins and needles! Sure, Concrete is an important invention, but I'm the backbone of modern engineering, have no doubt.

- ◉ Steel was first used around 4,000 years ago in Asia

- ◉ Iron is about 1,000 times weaker than steel

- ◉ Today, steel is the most widely used metal in the world

SAY WHAT?

Alloy: A metal made by mixing two or more metals together, or a metal and a nonmetal.
Coke: A hard fuel that's mostly carbon and is made when coal or oil is heated up.

TOP ENGINEER

In 1856 English inventor Sir Henry Bessemer found that blowing air through melted iron made it easier to pour. Steel might be strong, but American engineer Stephanie Kwolek made something even stronger in the 1960s: Kevlar. Five times stronger than steel, it's used in bulletproof vests!

Aluminum
★ Metal Molder

THE BIG IDEA

A soft and flexible metal, widely used in a number of everyday products around the world, including soda cans.

So you've met super-tough Steel, huh? Well, I'm Aluminum, a metal whose strengths lie in being light and flexible.

I often mix with other metals — say, copper, magnesium, tin, or zinc — to make alloys. At my purest, I am mined from an **ore** called bauxite and mixed with oxygen. Once this mix is crushed, it is possible to extract a solid called alumina from it. If you heat up alumina by running an electric current through it, you get molten aluminum — me — which you can then mold into sheets or things such as cans!

⊙ Around 200 billion aluminum cans are used globally each year

⊙ Almost 70% of aluminum cans are recycled. Many are made into new aluminum cans

SAY WHAT?

Ore: A material that occurs in the ground and from which metal or other minerals are extracted so that they can be used elsewhere.

⁎ APPLYING SCIENCE ⁎

Aluminum is molded into many useful everyday things, from forks and spoons to window frames, airplane parts, and even baseball bats!

Plastic

★ Shape Maker

THE BIG IDEA

A light but sturdy human-made material that can be molded into many different shapes and so has lots of uses.

Hey, I'm Plastic. You're going to say I'm bad for the planet, but hear me out before you decide for good. You see, I'm a super-useful **polymer** that's transformed the world.

I'm made from oil that's extracted from the ground and made into small pellets. Melted in a furnace, these pellets become liquid plastic, which can be molded into so very many different shapes, from chairs and trash cans to eyeglasses and bottles. The bad news is that it takes 1,000 years for me to decompose. The good news is that I can usually be recycled. But, to their shame, too many humans just throw me away!

- ⊙ About 480 billion plastic bottles were sold worldwide in 2016

- ⊙ Only 10% of plastic in the world is actually recycled

- ⊙ By 2050 the oceans will contain more pieces of plastic waste than fish

SAY WHAT?

Polymer: A substance within which many groups of atoms, called molecules, are stuck together. They can be natural (for example, wool) or human-made (for example, nylon).

TOP ENGINEER

Belgian chemist Leo Baekeland is often credited with starting the plastic era. In 1907 he created an early type of plastic called Bakelite. Since that time, many new types of plastic have been made, all based on his initial idea.

Ceramic
★ Super Solid

THE BIG IDEA

Any solid nonmetal material is called a ceramic. Pottery and porcelain are among the most familiar.

Wow! I am amazing! Sure, when you think of me, Ceramic, you might picture dinner plates, coffee cups, tiles, and even your toilet! But did you know Glass and Cement are classified as me? Yep, so are bricks and diamonds! That's because a "ceramic" is basically any solid object that isn't a metal.

The ceramics you are familiar with are made by mixing **clay** with water, shaping it into a pot or bowl, and letting it dry hard. Such objects have been used in one form or another by humans for thousands of years. They're some of the oldest human-made materials around! And some of the most beautiful in my humble opinion.

- ◉ The word "ceramic" comes from the Greek word *keramos*, which means pottery

- ◉ Ancient civilizations were making pottery up to 20,000 years ago

SAY WHAT?

Clay: A kind of earth that is soft when it is wet and hard when it is dry. It can be shaped and baked to make things.

APPLYING SCIENCE

One of the most basic ceramics is the building brick. In its simplest form, a brick is just a chunk of dried-out mud.

Textile

⭐ Wonder Weaver

THE BIG IDEA

Material made from weaving **yarn**. It is used to produce items of clothing, sheets, and other useful products.

You wear clothes, right? Then you know about me, Textile! I include many things that are knitted, woven, or sewn. I'm made of tiny things called fibers. Some fibers, such as cotton, come from plants, while others, such as wool, come from animals. Human-made (synthetic) fibers exist, too — you've probably heard of nylon and polyester.

Spin any fibers into yarn, and you can weave or knit with them to produce me. Dye the yarns first, and you'll end up with beautiful, colored textiles. Weave or knit with several different colored yarns, and you'll be able to create textiles with the most fantastic patterns.

- ◉ Wool is the world's most commonly used animal fiber

- ◉ Silk is produced by caterpillar-like insects called silkworms

⚡ **SAY WHAT?** ⚡

Yarn: Plant or animal fiber that has been spun to make an endless thread. It can be used for sewing, knitting, and weaving.

✳ **AGE-OLD WISDOM** ✳

There is evidence of textiles having been made as far back as 3000 BC. Cotton was used for the first time around 600 BC, and silk arrived on the scene in about AD 400.

Adhesive
★ Sticky Stuff

THE BIG IDEA

A **substance** that can stick two or more materials together. Adhesives are usually liquid, but they harden when exposed to air.

If getting sticky is your thing, hang out with me, Adhesive. I have no rivals when it comes to sticking stuff together. No doubt you use glue at school? Well then, we're best buddies already!

I'm useful because I start out as a liquid, but turn solid as I dry. I form a tight bond between two surfaces, which then find themselves stuck together. My friend Concrete uses a popular adhesive called cement to make its other ingredients stick together. Some adhesives, such as superglue, are mega strong. They suit all kinds of industrial purposes and can stick metals together in airplanes and cars.

- ◉ A dab of superglue measuring 1 × 1 in. (2.5 × 2.5 cm) could support the weight of a car

- ◉ You can make glue using the same ingredients that are used to make bread: flour, salt, and water

SAY WHAT?

Substance: Any type of matter made up of a single kind of chemical. Matter made up of two or more chemicals is called a mixture.

GREAT INVENTION

It is possible that adhesives were made around 200,000 years ago, when early humans used them to stick stones together! Around 70,000 years ago, people used them to make tools such as axes.

Graphene

★ Miracle Material

THE BIG IDEA

A super-thin substance that can be stacked together in sheets to produce a new material that's extremely light but very strong.

Some of my Cool Stuff pals have been around for centuries, but not me. No, I'm Graphene, brand spanking new and a "miracle" material to boot.

I'm made of super-thin sheets of **graphite** that are stuck together. How thin is super thin? Well, each sheet is just one atom thick! Yep, ultra thin. Layer lots of these sheets together and you get me, a material that's 200 times stronger than steel, but six times lighter! I'm so young that scientists are still exploring the uses I might have, but it seems I could play a big role in the future of medicine, electronics, energy storage, and oh so much more.

- ◉ Graphene is the thinnest material in the world

- ◉ A sheet of graphene as thick as paper could support an elephant

- ◉ Graphene is not only super strong, it's also almost transparent (see-through)

SAY WHAT?

Graphite: A nonmetallic material that's found in rocks and is quite soft and slippery. It's used in pencils and batteries.

TOP ENGINEERS

Scientists Andre Geim and Konstantin Novoselov first made graphene in 2004 in Britain. They used tape to strip away really, really thin layers from graphite, and then they stacked all the layers together.

Clean Water

Sanitation

Electrification

Refrigeration

Communication

Bicycle

Automobile

Bridge

Skyscraper

Computer

Space Tech

New Seeds

Renewable Energy

Mega Feats

You met the Specialists on pages 20 through to 41, and now it's time to get to know some of their fantastic feats of engineering. These groundbreaking types have really changed the world . . . or are about to. Clean Water, Sanitation, and Refrigeration save millions of lives by keeping nasty germs at bay. Bicycle, Automobile, and Space Tech have pushed the boundaries of exploration. And with New Seeds and Renewable Energy, it looks as if Earth's future could be brighter. Let's go meet the whole team and see what they're up to!

Clean Water
★ Thirst Quencher

THE BIG IDEA

Water that is safe to drink. Chemicals have been used to remove harmful **bacteria** from this water.

I'm one of the most amazing inventions of the modern world — Clean Water. I bet that surprises you, because I'm common in many places, but don't be fooled by that. Not everyone is so fortunate.

If you drank water in its basic form, you might get sick. It contains lots of bacteria, and some of them may be harmful. So my specialist pal Chemical Engineering treats water to make it safe to drink. What's more, that superhero is continually trying to come up with ways to clean water in poorer countries so that everyone can stay healthy.

- 780 million people in the world are without access to clean water

- 10% of people have to travel more than 30 minutes to fetch water

- By 2025, half of the world will struggle for water because of climate change

SAY WHAT?

Bacteria: Tiny organisms made of single cells. They are found everywhere on the planet. Some are bad for us and can make us sick if we inhale or swallow them.

* AGE-OLD WISDOM *

Both the ancient Romans and the ancient Greeks came up with ways to make water safe to drink. These included boiling the water to kill some harmful bacteria, and filtering the water through charcoal to make it healthier.

Sanitation

★ Super Sewer

You might find them gross, but toilets and sewers are my heroes. I'm Sanitation, one of Civil Engineering's great inventions. I make sure that all the waste that comes out of your body gets washed away so that there's no buildup of bacteria where you live, work, and play.

Flush your toilet, and all the waste travels down into a sewer below ground. This network of pipes leads to a treatment plant. The solid waste is separated from the liquid waste and gotten rid of (whew!). Meanwhile, chemicals kill off the bacteria in the liquid waste, leaving water that is safe to use on farms and in gardens.

- ◉ The first sanitation system is thought to have existed in northwest India around 4,000 years ago

- ◉ Around 2.4 billion people in the world are without a sanitation system

Electrification
★ Bright Dazzler

THE BIG IDEA

A feat of electrical engineering that involves using bulbs and electricity to produce light so that we can see in the dark.

On, off, on, off. Sure, lighting up your house is as easy as flipping a switch, but trust me, it's amazing! I'm Electrification, and you can thank me for lighting up the world around you. I'm just glowing with pride.

My roots date back to the 1800s, when scientists first discovered how to use electricity. But it wasn't until 1878 that the first light bulbs were invented. These **incandescent** light bulbs used a hot glowing wire to produce light. Modern light bulbs use an electronic gizmo called a light-emitting diode (LED) instead. Science has come a long way, but without me you'd still be in the dark!

- Before light bulbs, people used gas lamps to see at night

- It would take as many light bulbs as there are stars in the universe to match the brightness of the Sun

SAY WHAT?

Incandescent:
Something that emits light when it is heated up, such as a wire found in some light bulbs.

✳ TOP ENGINEERS ✳

American inventor Thomas Edison is known for making the first widely used light bulb in 1879. Around the same time, in 1878, British inventor Sir Joseph Swan came up with a similar idea. Thanks to both, light bulbs became common around the world!

Refrigeration
★ Super Cooler

THE BIG IDEA

A method of cooling down food to prevent the growth and spread of bacteria.

There's nothing worse than the smell (and taste) of sour milk. Rotting food makes a great home for bacteria. If you eat bad food, there's a chance you might get sick. Ha, not with me around! I'm Refrigeration, an amazing engineering feat that keeps food cool so it doesn't go bad.

Inside a refrigerator is a clever system of pipes filled with **refrigerant**. This super smart substance removes heat from the refrigerator, and keeps its insides nice and cold. The bacteria has less energy to grow, and the food lasts longer — not forever, though.

- The ideal temperature inside a refrigerator is 37.5°F–40°F (3°C–5°C)

- The refrigerator was first invented back in 1834, using ice instead of electricity

SAY WHAT?

Refrigerant: A substance used inside a refrigerator. It can change from liquid to gas and carries heat from inside a fridge to outside.

APPLYING SCIENCE

Another technique for storing food is canning. Food is placed inside a tin can or glass jar and heated until any bacteria dies. It is then sealed so no more bacteria can get in and grow. Canned food keeps much longer than fresh food.

Communication

★ Terrific Texter

THE BIG IDEA

Using electricity and radio waves to transfer information from one device to another, often across great distances.

If you've sent a text to someone far away, you'll have been using me, Communication! Before me, people sent physical messages via land, sea, and air. Just imagine that!

Your phone turns your text into an electrical **signal** and sends it to a nearby transmission tower. Radio waves ping the signal to a second transmission tower that's near the person you want to message. Their phone converts the signal to text again, and they can then read what you've said. Cool, no? With modern phones we can also send messages over the Internet. Feeling chatty?

- Around five billion people in the world have a cell phone

- People with cell phones check for messages every 12 minutes on average

SAY WHAT?

Signal: An electrical packet of data that is sent or received, such as the signal from a phone or the TV signal in your house.

TOP ENGINEERS

The Italian Antonio Meucci first invented a working phone in 1849. It wasn't until 1876 that Scottish-American inventor Alexander Graham Bell came up with the landline phone that we use today.

Bicycle
★ Pedal Power

THE BIG IDEA

A two-wheeled vehicle that is powered by a person pedaling. It uses **gears** to speed up and slow down.

Hi, I'm Bicycle, a vehicle with two wheels that is powered by pedaling. A feat of Mechanical Engineering, I have handlebars at the front, with levers and cables for operating my brakes and gears.

Usually, several gears attach to my rear wheel. A chain connects those gears to my pedals, so that one gear rotates when the pedals are pushed. This drives my wheels forward. By shifting gear size, you can change how much energy you need to put in to keep moving: the larger the gear, the easier it is to pedal (but the slower you will go).

- ◉ You can travel five times farther on a bike than walking while using the same energy

- ◉ The world's fastest bicycle ride was 184 mph (296 kmh) across the Bonneville Salt Flats in Utah

SAY WHAT?

Gear: A wheel with little ridges, or teeth, that can transfer power or energy from one source to another.

✳ GREAT INVENTION ✳

A basic pedal-powered vehicle with four wheels was invented in 1418. But the modern bicycle didn't emerge until the 1800s, with several people — including German Karl Kech and Frenchman Pierre Lallement — claiming to have invented it.

Automobile
★ Speedy Driver

THE BIG IDEA
A vehicle with wheels that can transport passengers and cargo from one place to another, often using an engine.

You've been in a car, but do you know how cars work? Well, I'm Automobile, a triumph of Mechanical Engineering.

I'm the go-to character for zipping from A to B. Basically a box on wheels, I normally rely on an engine to make my journeys. It's found in my front or back end and uses fuel (such as **gasoline**) to move pistons and rods. These then turn the wheels of the car to make it go forward and backward. Pressing my gas pedal sends more fuel into my engine, and I go faster. Modern versions of me use electricity-powered batteries instead of gasoline to turn my wheels.

- ◉ There are an estimated one billion cars in the world today

- ◉ The world's fastest car, the Koenigsegg Agera, can reach speeds of 277 mph (445 kmh)

SAY WHAT?

Gasoline: A product of petroleum. Petroleum is a form of oil taken from the ground. It forms when animals decay over millions of years and can be used as fuel.

TOP ENGINEER

The history of the car dates back to the first steam-powered vehicle, built in 1769. But it wasn't until 1885 that German engineer Karl Benz designed the first practical car that ran on gasoline.

Bridge
★ Holder Upper

THE BIG IDEA

A construction that allows people and vehicles to travel over a gap or body of water, by supporting a road or path above.

Want to cross a river without getting wet? Use me, Bridge! I'm a construction that can take people or vehicles from one side of a valley to another. If there's not a river below, maybe there's a road or a railroad.

Wow! There are so many different types of me. An **arch** bridge has curved supports to hold it up. A beam bridge — long and straight — is raised on columns or piers, while a suspension bridge uses Steel's cables to help carry the load! I look fantastic, I know, but I'm also a technical genius. Traffic needs to be able to get from one side of me to the other without me falling down!

- ◉ Modern drawbridges are made of two halves that swing up in the air to let boats pass through

- ◉ Hamburg, Germany, has 2,500 bridges — more than any other city in the world

SAY WHAT?

Arch: A curved structure that can support a large amount of weight above it.

GREAT INVENTION

China's Danyang-Kunshan Grand Bridge is the world's longest. It's an astonishing 102 miles (165 km) long, and it opened in 2011. It's used by trains. If it pointed upward, it would reach into space.

Skyscraper
★ Towering Triumph

THE BIG IDEA

A very tall modern **building**, usually found in a city.

What's that up in the sky? It's me, Skyscraper! With my head in the clouds, I'm one of the most amazing feats of engineering in history!

You have to be pretty special to be in my gang — taller than 490 ft. (150 m) for starters! I use those cool construction heroes Steel and Concrete to scale such heights. And Glass provides views far and wide from my windows. Underground, my deep foundations keep me from toppling over. Hey, don't worry if you see me wobble. In earthquake zones, I'm designed to move a little to absorb the shock.

- The first skyscraper was built in Chicago in 1884; it was ten stories tall

- The Burj Khalifa skyscraper in Dubai has 160 stories

- Hong Kong has over 300 skyscrapers, more than any other city

SAY WHAT?

Building: Any construction in which people live or work. They are often made of timber, brick, or steel and concrete.

* APPLYING SCIENCE *

Buildings like skyscrapers need heating and air-conditioning systems inside them to keep people warm or cool. They circulate air, and use heaters and fans to blow out hot or cold air.

Computer
★ Cool Calculator

THE BIG IDEA

A machine that is used for working with information. Users input commands and the computer performs them.

Don't pretend you don't know me! Computer? The most amazing machine of all time? Come on! I bet you use me to surf the Internet, but I can do way more than that.

When you use my mouse or keyboard to input an instruction, my **processors**, wires, and circuits work super fast to give you what you want. You'll see stuff appear on my monitor in no time. Some computers are big, but others are really small — a smartphone, for example. Now that I'm here (and getting smarter all the time), you'd be stuck without me.

- ◉ The first computer mouse was made out of wood in the 1960s
- ◉ There are more than two billion computers in the world today

⚡ SAY WHAT? ⚡

Processor: The "brains" of a computer. This is the part that takes an input and tells the rest of the computer what it needs to do with it.

✳ GREAT INVENTION ✳

The Internet is an incredible invention. It allows people to communicate all around the world, at great speed, sharing images and information. You can access the Internet on the World Wide Web, invented in 1989 by British scientist Tim Berners-Lee.

Space Tech

★ Ultimate Launcher

THE BIG IDEA

Various means of using devices in space so that they can explore the universe.

Dreaming of space travel? Take me with you. I'm Space Tech, the cool stuff engineers build to explore the **cosmos**.

Things usually kick off with a rocket, a spacecraft that uses huge amounts of fuel to launch straight up into space. Rockets carry satellites with them and release them into orbit around Earth. Satellites study the weather or help Communication send signals around our planet. Some rockets help space probes reach other worlds, such as Mars, so humans can learn more about them. And did you know there are astronauts actually living in space, on the International Space Station (ISS)?

- ◉ Space officially begins 62 miles (100 km) above Earth's surface

- ◉ There are more than 2,000 satellites orbiting Earth today

⚡ SAY WHAT? ⚡

Cosmos: Another term for the universe, the vast expanse of space between, and including, all the stars and planets. We see it spread out above us in the night sky.

✳ GREAT INVENTION ✳

The world's first satellite was Sputnik 1, which was launched into orbit by the Russians in 1957. It didn't do much besides emitting a noticeable radio beep, but it was the start of the exciting era of space exploration that we live in today!

New Seeds
★ Crop Saver

THE BIG IDEA

Engineering that alters the **DNA** of a crop to enable it to grow better in difficult conditions.

Many of the world's crops are threatened by drought (lack of water) and disease. With me, New Seeds, agricultural engineers hope to change this. I'm all about making crops stronger and longer-lasting by changing their DNA so that they can grow to have different abilities.

Some crops can be altered to love warm conditions, for example. Others can be changed to need less water, so that even if there is a drought, they can still grow. Many people in the world suffer from food shortages. With mega feats like me, engineers can aim to feed everyone.

- ◉ Rice is the most used crop in the world; most of it is grown in Asia

- ◉ Satellites help monitor the health of crops from space

- ◉ Africa is most at risk of crop shortages caused by climate change

SAY WHAT?

DNA: Material found in all organisms. It is made up of units called genes. Genes carry all the information that a living organism needs to grow, reproduce, and function.

✳ APPLYING SCIENCE ✳

Changing a crop's DNA is called genetic engineering. Corn and soy are two crops that have been genetically engineered.

Renewable Energy

★ Great Greener

Traditional forms of energy rely on fuels such as coal and oil. These pollute the air and can harm human health and the environment. Let me help! I'm Renewable Energy. Clean and green, I can be used over and over again.

Sunlight, wind, and energy from waves are all forms of me. They are "renewable" because they are always going to be available on our planet. They are capable of producing plenty of energy if used well. For example, solar panels can capture sunlight, and machines called turbines can make use of the wind and waves.

- ◉ One-fourth of the world's energy comes from renewables

- ◉ Geothermal power harnesses energy from hot water and steam found underground

Glossary

Adjustment: A small change that is made to something such as a machine or a process.

Alloy: A metal that is made by mixing two or more types of metals together.

Arch: A curved structure that can support a large amount of weight above it.

Bacteria: Tiny single-celled organisms that are found everywhere on the planet. Some are bad for us and can make us sick if we inhale or swallow them.

Breaking point: The maximum stress a material can take before it breaks apart.

Building: Any construction in which people live or work. Buildings are often made of timber, brick, or steel and concrete.

Cement: A mixture of limestone and clay. It creates a sticky glue-like paste when water is added to it.

Chemical: Any substance that is made up of matter. It can be a solid, a liquid, or a gas.

Chemistry: The study of matter and how it works, which often involves looking at elements and substances.

Circuit: A series of wires or conducting material that allows a current to move through it.

Clay: A kind of earth that is soft when it is wet and hard when it is dry. It can be shaped and baked to make things.

Climate change: The warming of the planet, mostly caused by the release of carbon dioxide from human-made power plants.

Coke: A hard fuel that's mostly carbon and made when coal or oil is heated up.

Constraint: Anything that limits what can be done or achieved when designing something.

Cosmos: Another term for the universe, the vast expanse of space between, and including, all the stars and planets. We see it spread out above us in the night sky.

Criteria: In research, what a design needs to do or achieve.

Crop: A plant that's grown in large quantities, usually for food. Fruits, vegetables, and cereals such as wheat are all types of crops.

Current: A flow of electricity through a wire or circuit. It transfers energy from one area of a device or system to another.

DNA: Material found in all organisms. It is made up of units called genes. Genes carry all the information that a living organism needs to grow, reproduce, and function.

Durability: A measure of how long something will last, often given in years or months depending on what the product is.

Efficiency: The good use of time and energy while performing a task.

Environment: Everything you can see around you in the natural world.

Fiber: A long, thin thread of a material, which can be either natural or human-made.

Field: An area of study that a person can be a specialist in, such as the field of biology or the field of chemistry.

Force: An amount of energy that causes an object to move in a certain direction when the force is applied.

Fossil fuel: A type of fuel that formed thousands or millions of years ago and is found in the ground. Oil and gas are fossil fuels.

Foundation: The part of a building that goes into the ground and that supports the entire weight of the building above it.

Full-scale model: A model that is exactly the same size as the real thing.

Furnace: A structure used for heating materials such as sand or iron to extremely high temperatures. A furnace is normally gas-powered.

Gasoline: A product of petroleum. Petroleum is a type of oil taken from the ground. It forms when animals decay over millions of years, and can be used as fuel.

Gear: A wheel with little ridges, or teeth, that can transfer power or energy from one source to another.

Graphic: An image that shows what a real-world object looks like, often made using computers.

Graphite: A nonmetallic material that's quite soft and slippery. It's used in pencils and batteries.

Green: Kind to the environment.

Incandescent: Something that emits light when it is heated up, such as a wire found in some light bulbs.

Infrastructure: All the human-made parts of civilization you can see around you, including buildings and roads.

Internet: A collection of computers around the world that share information. It allows people to communicate across large distances.

Magnet: A material that has its atoms ordered in a certain way to produce an attractive force known as magnetism.

Material: A chemical, or mix of chemicals, in the form of a solid object. Some materials are natural, but others can only be made by human beings.

MRI: Magnetic resonance imaging, a technique for forming pictures of the inside of the body.

Nano: A material that is really small — one nanometer is a millionth of a millimeter.

Ore: A material that occurs in the ground and from which scientists extract metal or other minerals to be used elsewhere.

Physics: The study of matter and energy in the universe, including things such as light and heat.

Plant fiber: Part of a plant made of cells, usually in the form of a thin thread. Lots of fibers joined together can be pressed to make paper.

Pollution: Substances that enter the environment and can be dangerous or harmful to plants and animals living there.

Polymer: A substance within which many groups of atoms, called molecules, are stuck together.

Process: A series of actions or steps taken in order to reach a particular result.

Processor: The "brains" of a computer. This is the part that takes an input and tells the rest of the computer what it needs to do with it.

Prosthetic: An artificial body part, such as an arm, a leg, or even a heart.

Prototype: A full-scale model that actually functions, so that engineers can test all aspects of the design.

Recycle: Taking something that would normally be thrown away as waste and finding another use for it. This sometimes involves breaking it down.

Refrigerant: A substance used inside a refrigerator. It can change from liquid to gas and carries heat from inside a fridge to outside.

Satellite: A machine that orbits Earth (or even another world), often used to take images of the planet or send communications around the globe.

Scaled-down: A version of something that is identical in every way but several sizes smaller.

Sketch: In engineering, a diagram or drawing that shows the various parts of a project you're hoping to build.

Solution: One possible answer to a given question or problem.

Substance: Any type of matter made up of a single kind of chemical. Matter made up of two or more chemicals is called a mixture.

Teflon: A material that prevents things from sticking, commonly used on frying pans and other household objects.

Timber: Wood that has been chopped down and prepared for use in construction.

Vehicle: A mode of transportation that carries people or cargo from one place to another, often using engines and wheels or another form of movement.

Yarn: Plant or animal fiber that has been spun to make an endless thread. It can be used for sewing, knitting, and weaving.

Index